The Queen & Mr Brown
A Day for Dinosaurs

James Francis Wilkins

Published by the Natural History Museum, London

For Lucie, Linus, Stella, Pia, Alexandros
and Her Majesty, with affection.
Especial thanks to Steve and Colin.

First published by the Natural History Museum
Cromwell Road, London SW7 5BD

Hardback edition
© Trustees of the Natural History Museum, London,
2013
Text and illustrations © James Francis Wilkins
ISBN 978 0 565 09325 9
reprinted 2014

Paperback edition
© Trustees of the Natural History Museum, London,
2014
Text and illustrations © James Francis Wilkins
ISBN 978 0 565 09354 9

A catalogue record for this book is available from the
British Library.

Reproduction by Saxon Digital Services
Printed in China by C&C Offset Printing Co., Ltd

The Queen drew back the curtains and looked out.

"Mr Brown, it's snowing!" she called. He padded to the window and propped his paws against the sill. Flakes of wet snow were falling like stones from the sky. It was grey, gloomy and unbearably miserable.

Thank heavens he was inside in the warmth!

"They're like blobs of cotton wool. Aren't they beautiful", she continued. Mr Brown could see no beauty. He saw only a horrible, wet, cold day.

The Queen was not deterred. "I think we'll visit the dinosaurs today", she said.

After breakfast she dressed Mr Brown and put on
her warmest coat. She would not let the weather
spoil her day off. They would make the best of it and
visit the dinosaurs at the Natural History Museum
in South Kensington.

They went out through the side entrance of the Palace.
Mr Brown shuddered. He hated snow, especially snow
like this. This was certainly not weather for a royal corgi!
But the Queen was insistent so he tucked his head into
his coat and stepped out cautiously.

The weather was no obstacle to the tourists. A group
of them stood gazing through the Palace railings.
The Queen sometimes felt like a monkey in a cage.
She half expected that they would try feeding her
peanuts one day.

The Queen and Mr Brown joined the lines of people
who were crossing the park. Some were on their way
to work, others to shop. They kept their heads down

against the weather and said little. It was like a
silent ballet. The Queen smiled at her little friend.
"It's a good day for dinosaurs, isn't it."

It took them half an hour to walk to the Museum, by which time Mr Brown was as miserable as the weather. He would have preferred to stay at home and watch television from a comfortable chair.

As they entered the Museum Mr Brown froze in his tracks. He had not been there before and had no idea what to expect. What he saw shocked him.

An immense dinosaur skeleton, stretching the length of
the entrance hall, peered down at visitors as they came in.
Mr Brown knew it was dead but he was taking no chances.

Even a dead dinosaur must be treated with extreme
caution. He tried to make himself small and pressed
close to the Queen.

They left their coats in the cloakroom and walked to the
Dinosaur Gallery. More giant skeletons stood in rows.
The Queen wondered what they had looked like when
they were alive, for no-one has seen a living dinosaur.

They lived long long ago, before there were people on the Earth, and they were the most powerful of all creatures. But then, for some strange reason, they all died out.

There were many types of dinosaur. Some, like Brachiosaurus, Diplodocus and Manenchisaurus, were vegetarian. They had very long necks so that they could eat from trees.

Others, like Megalosaurus, Carnotaurus and Tyrannosaurus rex, were ferocious meat-eaters. They had large heads and strong back legs for running after their prey.

Once Mr Brown had grown used to the skeletons he was quickly bored and wandered off by himself. But the Queen was fascinated. She wanted to understand everything and read all that there was to read.

She looked in awe at the model of a Tyrannosaurus rex.
It had teeth seven inches long in a mouth so big it
could have swallowed her whole. It was so realistic
it seemed to be alive.

She gazed in wonder at another display. It was the right foot of an Iguanodon which had suffered from arthritis one hundred million years ago, just like people do now. Nothing really changes, she thought.

And then she read how the dinosaurs had died out.
Scientists think that a gigantic rock fell from the
sky, stirring up so much dust that the sun was
hidden for three months. This caused the Earth to
become very, very cold. Too cold for dinosaurs.

This is probably what happened, but maybe...
just maybe...

they killed themselves by jumping off a cliff...

they were overwhelmed by the stink of their own poo...

they bored themselves to death...

or aliens came from outer space and ate them for breakfast.

As the Queen stood imagining the various possibilities, it occurred to her that she hadn't seen Mr Brown for a long time. She hurried off to search for him and found him fast asleep, stretched out in front of a huge bone.

He woke up and they looked at it together.

   "Left thigh-bone of an Apatosaurus", she read.
It was as tall as she was. Not even in his dreams
had Mr Brown imagined such a magnificent bone.

They had now spent half the day in the Museum and the Queen was beginning to feel tired. She sat down on a bench and ate a sandwich. She then fed Mr Brown some biscuits while she thought about all the things they had seen.

It was pleasantly warm in the Museum and it wasn't
long before she found herself nodding off to sleep.
Mr Brown flopped down next to her and closed
his eyes.

In the distance she could hear a noise, a familiar
noise, and one she loved to hear.

It was the sound of the crowd at Ascot, and they were chanting a name, over and over again. As she listened she suddenly realised that it was her name they were chanting. She was not watching a race, she was taking part in one!

Her mount was lunging forward with giant strides. Instinctively she urged it on, but it was such a powerful beast she had difficulty controlling it.

She had an even bigger shock when she glanced down. It was not a horse she was riding...

...it was a Megalosaurus! The giant creature was
pounding along, snorting out breath. And with
every footfall the ground shuddered and

she was jolted violently and nearly thrown from its back. The Queen was a good rider but she had never ridden a monster like this!

The crowd were chanting her name because she
was leading the race! But she hardly heard them as
she needed all her concentration to avoid being

thrown under the feet of the other dinosaurs.
They raced around the final curve of the track
and thundered down the home straight.

The finishing post was in sight and she dug her feet into the animal's side, spurring it on. She only had to keep going to be the winner and she liked winning!

But the crowd had started to chant another name and she could hear another dinosaur close behind her and getting closer. She glanced over her shoulder only to see...

...the tiny body of Mr Brown bouncing up and down like a ball on the back of a Carnotaurus. It was his name that the crowd was chanting now.

He was just as determined to win as the Queen was
and he held on doggedly until he was almost level
with her.

As they came up to the winning post, Mr Brown's
dinosaur dipped its head like a sprinter and crossed
the line inches ahead of the Queen's dinosaur.

The Queen could hardly believe it. She had been
pipped at the post by her best friend. It was just
too annoying!

The crowd surged excitedly around Mr Brown
and his Carnotaurus as it was led into the winner's
enclosure, sweating and steaming. Everybody
clapped and cheered and Mr Brown was ecstatic.

He sprang from his mount in a victory leap as he had seen it done on television, for he had spent many afternoons watching horse racing and knew all about it.

But what he did not know, until this moment, was the beautiful feeling of winning.

He was presented with the winner's trophy which had his name engraved on it, under those of the previous winners.

His joy was boundless and his stumpy little tail
just wouldn't stop wagging.

"Madam, we're closing now", said a friendly voice.
The Queen tried to focus her thoughts and looked
up to see a Museum attendant smiling down at her.

"Dear me, I must have been sleeping", she said as
she got to her feet.

"I'll show you to the exit", he said and walked along beside them. "I don't blame you for coming in here in this weather", he continued, "I hope you've got a nice, warm home to go back to?"

"Thank you, yes yes, I do. That's very kind of you to enquire", she replied, quite touched by his concern.

The weather outside was now truly atrocious, with driving
snow. Mr Brown struggled through the slush and icy
puddles. His stubby little legs were not designed for this.

The Queen remained strangely silent. For some funny reason, perhaps wounded pride, she did not feel like telling him about her dream.

But eventually she did say something. "I wonder why the dinosaurs really did die out?"

Mr Brown grimaced. Sometimes he just did not understand her. If he had been able to speak he would have screamed out "IT'S BECAUSE THEY WENT OUT IN WEATHER LIKE THIS!"

But he kept quiet and thought of his warm basket waiting for him back at the Palace.

29664639R00024

Made in the USA
San Bernardino, CA
25 January 2016

Personalized "A Taste of Hebrew" Books
for English Speaking Kids
Perfect Party Favors

www.mazorbooks.com/HebrewBirthday.htm

Check Out the MazorBooks Library
Children's Books with Good Values

www.MazorBooks.com

www.mazorbooks.wordpress.com

www.facebook.com/mazorbooks

www.twitter.com/mazorbooks

More "A Taste of Hebrew" Books for English Speaking Kids

Counting in Hebrew for English Speaking Kids

A beautifully illustrated book that teaches kids to count in Hebrew from one to ten.

In *Counting in Hebrew* the numbers are written in Hebrew and in English as well as in English transliteration of the numbers and the Hebrew words that appear in this volume. The book also includes charts that teach Hebrew for cardinal numbers (1,2,3...) and ordinal numbers (1st, 2nd, 3rd...).In addition, the singular and plural versions of all the Hebrew words in the book are listed as well.

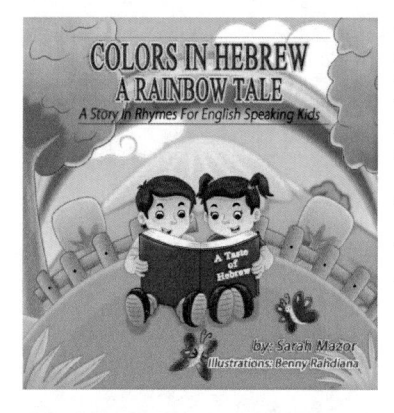

Colors in Hebrew: A Rainbow Tale

Kids of all ages are invited to journey with the sightseeing rainbow that travels to Israel and learns the names of fourteen colors in Hebrew.

The names of the colors are written in Hebrew with English transliteration and translation. For correct pronunciation check the transliteration chart that is included book.

Animals in Hebrew: A Day at the Zoo

Ami and Tami visit a zoo and learn the Hebrew names for animals.

Each one of the animals that is introduced in this lovely book is illustrated beautifully and appears with its English and Hebrew monikers and a little story in rhymes that describes its specific characteristics. Every page also presents the names of the animals in Hebrew letters and English transliteration, along with pronunciation help when necessary. Charts at the end of the book list all the animals that are mentioned (and illustrated) in the book in the order of their appearance in the story, both in English and in Hebrew.

Introduction to Hebrew: The Ancient and the Modern

The Hebrew language, the language of the Bible, was spoken by the Jews of the Land of Israel in ancient times and continued to serve as the language of prayer and study through the generations. The language was revived and reintroduced into the daily life of the Jewish population of Israel in the late 1800s by Eliezer Ben-Yehuda, the father of Modern Hebrew. Hebrew is the official language of the State of Israel.

Modern Hebrew accommodates the advent of societal, environmental and cultural evolution as well as the new scientific understanding, technological development and new-age innovation. Though Hebrew words are available for modern-day phenomena, English, Latin and other international words infiltrated the contemporary Hebrew-speaking individual's vocabulary, with words such as telephone, television, bacteria, or autobus, to name a few. However, Hebrew language purists and lovers of the ancient yet living language are cognizant of the fact that Hebrew words exist for modern innovation and that they are often based on the roots of words that are found in the Bible.

For example, the Hebrew word for computer is MACHSHEV. Its root of CHET/SHIN/VET is the same for CHOSHEV, a thinker (n.) or thinks (v.). LACHSHOV is to think and MACHSHEVON is a calculator.

Another example: The Hebrew word for train is RAKEVET and for vehicle is RECHEV, both share the root of REISH/CHAF/VET, ride, which is also the root of ROCHEV, a rider (n.) or the act of riding (v.). The roots REISH/CHAF/VET (רכב) and CHET/SHIN/VET (חשב) are Biblical in origin.
-Note: The BET and VET are the same letter as are the KAF and CHAF.

The Hebrew Alphabet: Silent Letters

There is only one official 'silent' letter in the Hebrew alphabet, the ALEPH. However, in modern-day Israel the letter AYIN is regarded as silent by many. The letter HEI is sometimes silent as well.

The ALEPH - א

Words written in Hebrew do not begin with a vowel (unlike English, where vowels are often found in the beginning of a word, as in - 'as' and 'in'). The one exception is the conjunction 'VAV' - as in UGA U'GLIDA, cake and ice cream. The symbol for the vowel 'U' in Hebrew is 'VAV' with a dot in its belly and when placed before a word it denotes the conjunction 'and'.

When Hebrew words begin with the sound of a vowel, like ADAM, the silent ALEPH is there to hold the vowel. When the ALEPH does not hold a vowel, which occurs in the middle or end of some words, then it is silent. For example, ABBA, father, is spelled ALEPH, BET, ALEPH (אבא)- Note that the first ALEPH holds the vowel 'aa' but the second is silent.

The AYIN - ע

Though the AYIN is not really silent, as it does have a sound that also exists in the Aramaic and Arabic languages, most Ashkenazi Jews and a growing number of Sephardi Jews treat the AYIN as they do the ALEPH. Silent. Nowadays it is acceptable to treat the AYIN as if it were silent.

The Letter HEI - ה

The HEI sounds like 'h' in 'honey'. However, when the HEI appears at the end of the word without a vowel, it is silent. For example, the Hebrew word for love is A-HA-VA (אהבה), spelled ALEPH, HEI, VET, HEI. The first HEI is pronounced (HA), the second HEI that appears at the end of the word is silent.

The Hebrew Alphabet: Interesting Facts

Hebrew is different than English in sound and also in the way it is written.
- The Hebrew alphabet has 22 letters, the first of which is aleph followed by bet.
- Five of the 22 letters are written a bit differently when they appear at the end of a word. They are the Kaf Sofit, Mem Sofit, Nun Sofit, Fei Sofit, and Tzadi sofit. (Sofit is from the word sof, which means final.)
- Some Hebrew letters have more than one sound. For example, the sound of 'P' and the sound of 'F' are represented by the same letter, pronounced 'Pei' or 'Fei' depending on the word. Hebrew vowels are represented by symbols, which generally are not written in texts though they are used in prayer books and beginner's learning books.
-The most observable distinction between Hebrew and the western languages is that Hebrew is written and read from right to left.

The first book of the 'A Taste of Hebrew for English Speaking Kids' series - focuses on the Hebrew alphabet.

In *The Hebrew Alphabet Book of Rhymes* the 22 letters of the alphabet are illustrated and spelled out in English and in Hebrew. In addition to the letters, 22 basic Hebrew words that are appropriate for young children are taught in a fun way. The words that are selected, one for every Hebrew letter, are written in Hebrew, transliterated and translated into English and depicted with an attractive illustration. Proper pronunciation help is provided with a 'sounds like…' example. Finally, each Hebrew word included in the book is incorporated into a sweet English rhyme that helps kids and adults recognize the Hebrew alphabet and learn foundational words in this beautiful language.

Have fun learning Hebrew!

More Hebrew for Beginners

You now know the twenty-two letters of the Hebrew alphabet or as they are known: The alephbet. You have also learned twenty-two basic words in Hebrew. But here are a few more that you might like to know!

(Use the transliteration table in the front of the book)

SHALOM means peace and it is also the way Hebrew speakers greet each other when they meet and when they say goodbye.

ISH is a man
ISHA is a woman

YELED is a boy
YALDA is a girl

ABBA is a father
IMMA is a mother

BEN is a son
BAT is a daughter

SABA is a grandfather
SAVTA is a grandmother

ACH is a brother
ACHOT is a sister

Be on the lookout for more 'A Taste of Hebrew for Kids' children's books. You may contact us with questions at:
Info@MazorBooks.com

ת

tav תּו

tinok - תִּינוֹק

_____

baby

Tiny little Tami is full of happiness and joy
Mommy is bringing home **TINOK**, a little baby boy

shin שִׁין

shokolad - שוקולד
_____
chocolate

Tiny little Shmuel is swell and dandy
Grandma gives him SHOKOLAD, his favorite candy

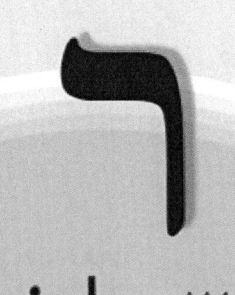

reish רֵישׁ

rakevet - רַכֶּבֶת

_____

train

Tiny little Rafi loves to travel far
He prefers the RAKEVET to riding in a car

ק

kuf קוף

kumkum - קומקום
_____

kettle

Tiny little Kobi loves to grow some seeds
Instead of boiling tea his KUMKUM waters weeds

tzadi צדי

tzaftzefa - צפצפה
—————————————
whistle

Tiny little Tzipi pretends she is a coach
She blows a **TZAFTZEFA** when the little kids approach

פ

pei פא

pil - פיל
_____
elephant

Tiny little Pnina has a grand imagination
She dreams of riding a PIL on an African vacation

ayin עִין

uga - עוּגה
_____

cake

Tiny little Adina has a real sweet tooth
Yet she shares her UGA with her best friend, Ruth

samech סמך

sus - סוס
_____
horse

Tiny little Sima loves her daddy's fables
Tales about a **SUS** who is living in his stables

nun   נוּן

naknikiya - נקניקיה

hot dog

Tiny little Nili who is a fussy eater

Loves a **NAKNIKIYA** so there's no need to feed her

mem מם

matana - מתנה
_____

present

Tiny little Moshe is now four years old
He gets a MATANA with ribbons red and gold

lamed למד

leitzan - ליצן
_____
clown

Tiny little Leah is a very funny girl
She dresses as a **LEITZAN** with a red nose and a curl

kaf כּף

kelev - כלב

dog

Tiny little Kineret asks for a puppy every day
When Mommy buys a **KELEV**, she cheers "hurray!"

yud   יוד

yalda - ילדה
_____
girl

Tiny little Yael is incredibly mature
She's a 3-year-old YALDA but people think she's four

tet טית

traktor - טרקטור

tractor

Tiny little Tali loves living on a farm

She's careful on a TRAKTOR and keeps away from harm

chet חית

chatul - חתול

cat

Tiny little Chaim loves his little pet
He cares for his CHATUL and takes him to the vet

zayin זַיִן

zayit - זַיִת
_____

olive

Tiny little Zevi is very very smart
He knows that olive oil is made from a ZAYIT's soft part

vav וו

vered - ורד

rose

Tiny little Varda named for a rose
Loves the smell of VERED that tickles her nose

הא hei

hipopotam - היפופוטם
hippopotamus

Tiny little Hodaya is visiting the zoo
And hears the HIPOPOTAM sneezing a-ha-achoo

dalet דלת

dubi - דובי

teddy bear

Tiny little Danny wants his pet in his bed
Mom gives him a DUBI to sleep with instead

ג

gimel גימל

glida - גלידה
_____
ice cream

Tiny little Gadi who is a good little boy
Decides he wants GLIDA instead of a toy

bet   בית

buba - בובה

doll

Tiny little Bina is performing today
With her favorite BUBA in the school's play

aleph אלף

aviron - אוירון
airplane

Tiny little Avi wants to fly up high
And from the AVIRON wave to all goodbye

The Hebrew Alphabet

in

Pictures and Rhymes

Guide to Transliteration

a :   as in barn

e :   as in sled

o :   as in go

i :   as in me

u :   as in glue

ei : as in day

tz : as in pretzel

ch : as in Loch Ness

or the sound you make
when clearing your throat

The Sounds of the Hebrew Letters

ALEPH sounds like the 'a' in arm*	LAMED sounds like the 'l' in lemon
BET sounds like the 'b' in buttons	MEM sounds like the 'm' in mommy
VET sounds like the 'v' in vest**	NUN sounds like the 'n' in nursery
GIMEL sounds like the 'g' in games	SAMECH sounds like the 's' in story
DALET sounds like the 'd' in doll	AYIN sounds like the 'a' in alligator*
HEI sounds like the 'h' in happy	PEI sounds like the 'p' in play
VAV sounds like the 'v' in violet	FEI sounds like the 'f' in flower**
ZAYIN sounds like the 'z' in zoo	TZADI sounds like the 'tz' in pretzels
CHET sounds like the 'ch' in Bach***	KUF sounds like the 'k' in kitten
TET sounds like the 't' in toy	REISH sounds like the 'r' in ribbon
YUD sounds like the 'y' in yellow	SHIN sounds like the 'sh' in shoes
KAF sounds like the 'k' in kite	SIN sounds like the 's' in sky**
CHAF sounds like 'ch' in Loch Ness**/***	TAV sounds like the 't' in television

*As both the Aleph and the Ayin are silent letters, they take on the sound of the vowel that
accompanies them. The vowel 'patach' - which sounds like 'aa' - is used in the example for Aleph.

** Alternate sound of same letter (bet/vet, kaf/chaf, pei/fei, and shin/sin).

*** The 'CH' sound is like the noise made when clearing one's throat.

The Hebrew Alphabet

ד dalet	ג gimel	ב vet	בּ bet	א aleph
ט tet	ח chet	ז zayin	ו vav	ה hei
★	ך chaf sofit	כ chaf	כּ kaf	י yud
	ם mem sofit	מ mem	ל lamed	★
ע ayin	ס samech	ן nun sofit	נ nun	
ץ tzadi sofit	צ tzadi	ף fei sofit	פ fei	פּ pei
ת tav	שׂ sin	שׁ shin	ר reish	ק kuf

The aleph and the ayin are silent letters. They both take the sound of the vowel that accompanies them. These vowels look like lines and dots that usually appear beneath the letter. The hei too is usually silent when it appears at the end of a word.

In This Book

- The Hebrew Alphabet Chart

- The Sounds of Hebrew Letters

- Guide to Transliteration of Hebrew Words

- The Hebrew Alphabet in Pictures and Rhymes

- More Hebrew for Beginners

- **More About Hebrew:**

-     Interesting Facts

-     Silent Letters

-     A Bit of History: The Ancient and the Modern

AUTHORS' NOTE

AUTHORS' NOTE

Did you know that bilingual children are better at problem solving? This is one of many benefits for exposing your children to more than one language. Multilingual-kids have also been found to be better at learning, planning and self-control.

Teach your kids Hebrew and enhance your children's development while you also provide them (and you) with a lifelong connection to the Bible and to Israel.

The Hebrew Alphabet: Book of Rhymes for English Speaking Kids is the first in the MazorBooks series of 'A Taste of Hebrew for Kids'. Look out for additional books in the series.

Shalom!

Sarah Mazor
Yael Rosenberg

Please note: Though the Hebrew language is read from right to left, this book, which is primarily written in English, is designed accordingly and should be read from left to right.

THE HEBREW ALPHABET
Book of Rhymes for English Speaking kids

YAEL ROSENBERG

SARAH MAZOR

Cover Illustration Raiza Pascual